A LONELY GRANDMOTHER

Also by Diane Moore

POETRY
Between Plants and Humans
Night Offices
Departures
In a Convent Garden
Mystical Forest
Everything is Blue
Post Cards From Diddy Wah Diddy
Alchemy
Old Ridges
Rising Water
The Holy Present and Farda
Grandma's Good War
Afternoons in Oaxaca (Las Poesias)
The Book of Uncommon Poetry
Counterpoint
Your Chin Doesn't Want to Marry
Soaring
More Crows
Just Passing Through
Moment Seized

YOUNG ADULTS
Martin and the Last Tribe
Martin Finds His Totem
Flood on the Rio Teche
Sophie's Sojourn in Persia
Kajun Kween
Martin's Quest

ADULT FICTION
Redeemed by Blood
Silence Never Betrays
Chant of Death with Isabel Anders
Goat Man Murder
The Maine Event
Nothing for Free

CHILDREN
The Beast Beelzebufo
The Cajun Express

NON-FICTION
Porch Posts with Janet Faulk-Gonzales
Iran: In A Persian Market
Their Adventurous Will
Live Oak Gardens
Treasures of Avery Island

A LONELY

GRANDMOTHER

&

Other Poems

Diane Marquart Moore

BP

Sewanee, Tennessee

To Grandmother Nell

I

THE AGING EXPRESS

The sound of so many journeys
passes in the whistle of a train.
Little wonder this master of navigation
wails, pushing through sleeplessness
and darkness without news.

Shut-in passengers urge it on
thinking it a boundary-less machine
traveling on an open frontier
carrying them past houses with open windows
crying 'welcome aboard'
and rumbling through the night
making connections
in desolate places...
but not stopping for long.

A LONELY GRANDMOTHER

Someone stole one of my poems
and it emerged as a message
in a bottle on a TV show,
lines about loneliness
all bottled up
and floating into fame,
while I remained obscure.

As I watched the show,
I thought about Grandmother Nell
who lived beyond Grandfather Paul
twenty six years, all bottled up
in one bedroom of a Victorian manor,
ignoring the mold, faded wallpaper,
carpets without nap,
robed in the smocks she had sewn
for herself half a century,
except on Sundays
when no one at First Baptist Church
outdid her gloved finery.

She lived in that one room,
safe from the noise
of others' disapproval.
A snaggle-toothed space heater
blasted warmth she needed
for sieges of bronchitis,
Luden cough drops on the bureau,
her hands raw with eczema,
reading the tangible comfort
of her Bible, writing long letters
to distant relatives too sick to travel.

My aunt gave her a television set
the last years of her lonely life —
a window on the antics
of daytime preachers
who paced up and down
bellowing threats of a damned future
worse then her dark loneliness.

Her youngest daughter lived next door,
another, up the street,
but she preferred the closeted room
where she wore the overcoat of memory,
attached to no one,
loneliness past its limit,
the absence of light surpassing
the boundaries of silence
where she tried to feel something
beyond the lowered shades
of separation and sorrow.

II. WHAT THE ASSEMBLY LINE WROUGHT

She lived in certain prosperity 30 years,
Henry Ford's fledgling company
bringing her husband Paul
the Model T, Model A, "Motor Sales" —
a revolution in economics.
One in every six Americans,
employed by Ford Motor Company,
symbol of industrial capitalism.

She had a maid, a yardman,
sometimes a cook,
was chauffeured to New Orleans
once a month to visit relatives,
always in a new car.

Life was good...
then World War II erupted.

The roof of the Victorian house
and the "Garage"
(another name for Motor Sales)
began to leak in too many places,
Bright's Disease struck
and Paul's savings dissolved.
Ford cancelled his dealership,
the thick recordings
of "Henry's Made A Lady Of Lizzie,"
once played on a wind-up Victrola,
was scratched beyond repair.

They had danced to Ford's tune

and Paul died by it.
She drove a '47 Ford coupe
for 20 more years,
lived on boiled eggs and toast,
resigned herself to chance
and dumped the cracked record,
rented out part of the house
hoping to survive a dead end:
the century of modernism,
a time of mechanical madness.

SHE LEFT PART OF HERSELF WITH ME

and was intentional about it.
The smell of lavender lingers
in my bathroom closet,
the vision of her pursed mouth
willing me to a happy childhood.
I am still happy
thinking of the dusty cushion
of her love;
clean part in raven hair,
brisk steps clicking down the hall
searching for me
in my attic hideout
where the ghost of great-grandfather
found me and sent me into her arms.

She wore spectacles with gold rims
that fogged up as she dusted
the marble bust of Mozart
atop a bookcase of inherited volumes;
the green wool rug
stretched out like a cool sea,
marble-topped hall table,
ancient settees filling the room
with a civilized look I loved
and sank into its coolness.

In the afternoon,
an Emerson fan churned the air
of the sleeping porch
where I read until drowsy,
the hum of a sawmill up the street
like a faucet dripping monotony...

and serenity.

She was a decent, private woman
who seldom spoke affection,
on summer mornings gave me a broom
to sweep the front gallery,
never the back porch
for she cared about looking good,
a round bed of velvet pansies
in her front yard
attesting to the show.

When I cannot sleep
I think of her,
and I am happy again.
Had she lived into this future
she would have been 124,
still sewing pinafores with lambs
embroidered on the bodices
and cooking striped butterbeans
for great-great grandchildren.

She was always thinking
of keeping me as cool
as dotted Swiss in the summer,
and when I returned to my mother,
she sent union-suits for the dreaded cold,
a woman of mustard plasters,
Mentholatum up the nose,
Alka-Seltzer for stomach aches;

a small town grandmother
with a worn-out heart who said
"Your family is like
a tempest in a teapot,"
anxious that her oldest grandchildren

might not return another summer,
living, as they did,
on the precipice of alcoholism and poverty
with that bad-tempered German
and her daughter, my mother...
who did not survive the tempest.

STERN MORALS

Gray daylight filters
through subterranean chambers,
rain blurring the window.

She looks out at dead branches,
a jar of Mentholatum in hand,
waiting to soothe some grandchild's chest,
too late now to call up their names,
the beauty of their voices answering.

The room is filled with photos,
faces that don't speak,
her own lips unmoving.
She tries to sort out the absolutes
she had flung at them,
a cluster of Ben Franklin aphorisms,
proverbs from the Bible
closed on a bedside table,
the bald silence of a drafty room
now telling her, the children gone,
Absolutes will not keep her company.

SUMMER AFTERNOON

In the yard of wild fern
a pear tree grew,
the pears, almost brown,
sick and pebbly skin,
lay at the foot of a swing
near the chicken yard,
the smell of fertility drifting
out toward me.
I glimpsed two chickens pecking each other.

I wore a starched pinafore
Grandmother had sewn for me,
the sleeves with peaked shoulders
like small ears
and a sash binding my innocence.
When I bent to pick up a fallen pear
my grandparents rushed out,
leaving the kitchen table bare,
yelling for me not to eat the fruit
as if I were in the Garden of Eden
and forbidden fruit had fallen.

The tree with its large heart
had rained down unripe pears.
They covered the summer grass
thick and stiff with disapproval.
I turned the pear over in my hand
and bit into the leathery skin.
My childhood fled
before my grandparents' eyes.
Knowledge entered with a silent scream.
I knew I would no longer
live on the scent of innocence.

THE FAMILY BUSINESS

Ebenezer, the stone of help,
an Old Testament character
for whom Grandfather named
an outdoor kitchen he designed:
a wood structure with roof,
chimney, a roasting grill,
and on the chimney's side, an oven
with a temperature gauge —
modernity during World War II.

It was an artless shed,
symbol of his desire
to bring harmony to his families
who would picnic there,
declaring love,
revealing smiles with shark's teeth,
fresh from an attic of Nazis
hiding scarred souls
and the red dust
of undeclared domestic war.

The green-latticed kitchen
was much unused,
except as a grand space
for children's tea parties,
summer hunger, undisguised greed.
But it was also a retreat house
where Grandfather smoked his pipe,
struggling with pain and fatigue,
the politics of a small southern town,
talking about his fear
Ford Motor Company
would never produce cars again,

the war having taken away
his wealth and will to sell.

Ebenezer, an old Bible story
Grandfather thought he had housed
to triumph over family greed,
but his war, their war, never ended,
the bill came due too early for him,
and the franchise ended.
His offspring, still screeching,
clutched their wallets,
complaining about the lack
of his legacy to them,
while Ebenezer rotted to the ground,
leaving the chimney and an oven
with a modern temperature gauge
standing in the charged air of cold war,
an affront to the shed's ancient name.

DIFFERING PHILOSOPHIES

I crossed the little bridge spanning a ditch in the side yard
—a bucked-up, green-painted structure Grandfather had built
for us—and kicked at the spoiled pears lying on the parched
grass. We were soon gathered at the Thanksgiving table, rich
food laid out on a damask cloth in the dim dining room. The
chimneys had been boarded up and no cheerful smoke rose
from the rooftop. The family was grouped in silence around the
table, and after the long blessing, the impulse to ridicule Aunt
Kathryn's sugarcoated prayer overcame me.

"You remind me," I said, "of the Steig cartoon—a horse
with blinders on either side and the caption underneath
reading, 'Idealist.'"

Her lips pursed, a wild cat in her usually benign eyes, and
shot back: "Beauty is in the eye of the beholder."

She was a favorite aunt, and I don't know why I made the
remark, but the secret centers in both of us had been exposed.
The blood of kin splattered on the Noritake china; the moment
became a permanent break.

Last night I dreamed of this aunt. I was cleaning her tiny
house on Tenth Avenue, sorting accumulations of unjust
remarks as I worked. It was Thanksgiving again, and my aunt
entered the kitchen. A man who had been fishing with my
Uncle Tony brought in a mess of large, green-looking bass. I
had thrown away the containers that might have held them,
and my aunt was not happy with me.

"Take them away," she told me. "They are ugly and smell."

I threw the fish and the riposte at her, "Beauty is in the eye of the beholder."

Her eyes were not benign; our hearts had made no progress.
"You," she said, "do not know how to live without trouble."

I woke up to redeeming darkness.

ANGEL IN THE HALL

A cherub's face
engraved on a brass lamp

danced on her toes,
holding out changeless arms,

an embrace we rushed past
in the dark hall of loneliness,

fleeing the hint of bondage
hammered into her smile.

The cherub had lost illumination
and any messages from heaven

she might have brought to earth,
having flown great distances

to impart wisdom or strength,
or simply a quiver of joy.

Grandmother kept her rooted there,
the illusion of a happier past:

moments of light glowing
at Thanksgiving and Christmas,

children opening French doors
exposing a lone piece of art,

shadows departing
in her old Victorian house.

A cupola with stained glass window
stared out at the dusty street

where few cars passed,
their drivers unaware

of the radiant being,
a flicker of light trapped indoors

in a piece of brass
fixed in solitary confinement,
Grandmother keeping her there,
imagining awakening

to this celestial light...

A DETERMINANT OF POSITION

Don't look down
was the command she snapped
while measuring a hem
on one of many dresses
she sewed for me
from birth until I married.
Don't look down
at my gray and scaly knees,
suspend my talking
and stand up straight,
lord, she was General Patton in disguise.

Don't look down
had its various meanings
like *hold up your head,*
keep your back straight,
and, to her, they all meant *Be Proud,*
although I redefined their limitations:
Don't Be.
Don't look down,
shame might swallow you whole
or someone might call you common.
God forbid.

She was a little country girl,
married a Mississippi sawmill baron,
a man descended from Scots gentry
with a literary bloodline,
one of the Hume clan
elevated beyond her class.
But their blood was thin and puny
and she outlived him by thirty years,
longevity which would have made her proud.

The dresses she fashioned for me,
those brilliant Scottish plaids,
were always eye catchers,
clothing that turned people's heads,
each stitch a witness to her pride,
dresses that made them anxious
their own garments
might be common when compared
to my finely-stitched apparel,
about which we were always able
to hold up our heads,
never had to look down,
her measurements so exact.

MAKING FACES

It was only a small grimace
I returned for the tongue extended
at me for an instant,
then retracted as quickly
as the lizards my brother tortured.
She had made the gesture
for no reason,
except, perhaps she suffered
from a spasm of jealousy
because I made good grades.
And she did not.

Miss Williams caught only my grimace
a half-hearted retaliation,
this slight breach of etiquette,
but she allowed no trespass.
Until then, the red-haired teacher
had been my idol,
the fourth person I had added
to the Holy Trinity.

I had wished for prolonged applause
from her, but now she said,
"Come up and stand before the class
and make that face again."
I was two desks away from humiliation,
walked to the front of the room,
bowed my head and grimaced.
It was my second humiliation
at Nicholson Public School,
the first, an accident
of passing water on the front steps
too afraid to ask directions

to what we called "The Girls' Basement."

Two humiliations at a school
I revered,
the smell of chalk dust
talcum powder on my shyness,
shelves of books
about children in foreign lands,
a reward for excellence in reading,
my life enclosed in a library rail.
Recess was a dreaded disturbance.
I never wanted to leave the room
of words, numbers, colors,
books Miss Williams passed to me.
But something shattered that day,
I sobbed aloud, felt cold inside
with the first-born mistrust of an idol,
an encounter with unfairness
that covered the sun for months.

Oh, the hard test of humiliation,
one that kept me silent in groups
until I was twenty-three
and another red-haired woman
invited me to the head of a class,
where I found my tongue,
one I should have stuck out
at Ann Fortner, a name engraved
on my shit list forever.

That day when the last bell rang
and we filed out through the cloak room,
Miss Williams extended her arms.
"Come give me a hug," she said,
"I know you're really a good girl."
It was the same refrain as

my grandmother's last words to me,
"Be sweet now."
I succumbed to Miss Williams' arms,
knowing she hadn't meant well,
and the world would have to grow larger,
she, nor any other flaming-haired pedagogue
would gain my obeisance again.

THE NIGHT RAINED ACORNS

Shiny green bullets
struck the rooftop,
a watchful squirrel
drooping with insomnia
garnering them
when they rolled off
onto the parched grass.

Grandmother showed them to me
when I was four,
told me not to dare
put them in my mouth.
When she went indoors
I gathered a crop
of the cup-shaped fruit,
stomped on one
with a white cowboy boot
and lifted out the orange mast,
the first taste
of rebellion against her,
bitter in my mouth,
bitter as a cup of hemlock.

Today a wind came,
tumbling the leaves
of a white oak
more acorns raining down.
I saw a woodpecker
stealing a giant nut
from a gray squirrel,
daring him to touch
the stolen cargo.
Black and red in flight,

laden with bounty,
his primitive hunger
buoyed him higher
than the tallest oak.

I wondered if the first taste
of his stolen prize
would be as bitter
as the sting
of my early disobedience,
or, if in his emancipated world,
stealing is a legal act,
and his grandmother
had allowed him the bitterness
of his own mistakes.

II

MUSHROOMS

At first when I saw them
I was struck by their brilliance,
the round orange heads,
strangers without bodies
glowing in dead grass
and a disagreeable gloom —
visitors no longer in hiding
beneath the paternal shelter of trees.

Later, when they split open,
some toppling over
like tipsy old ladies,
the smell overcame me,
death on patrol.
Rot, nourishing the roots of oaks —
rot, not unlike human decay
in a graveyard surrounded by trees,
but the mushrooms
were without markers
to announce they had passed,
the smell soon dissipating
as if they had never been,
only these lines I write remaining,
marking their time on my lawn,
diffident about their worth,
save as flashes of wonder
in a world of black flies.

MY LIFE REVIEW

lies in dreams,
dust collected under the bed,
thick with faces I mistrusted
and smelling of dirty laundry,
detritus I'd as soon forget,
but relentless in subterranean action.

Beneath the surface
there are old sea turtles
lying on the floor of the psyche
taunting me,
daring me to take them
back to life,
disturb my safety
between the walls
that try to keep out
a lingering sickness,
a blizzard of madness.

IDENTITIES

Every person
here
is from
somewhere else,
and,
having come
from *there*,
is happy
being *no one*
here
for *awhile*.
But soon
no one
wants to
become *someone else*
and settles
into being
anyone
from *elsewhere*.

GIVING UP ON LIFE

I am far from my family,
my brother, my daughters,
my cousins,
and all sentimental attachments
returning in my dreams,
I wonder if they care
as much as I do,
remembering vacation trips made,
dinners shared, laughter groping
for life's small pleasures.

I seem to be different,
caring beyond what I can care for
and I am haunted by derision,
is it my father laughing
or my mother screaming,
who knows
except the universe of feeling
reeling inside this cage
of no stars, just before dusk
sitting on a porch of exile
watching a turtle
hunched in the yard
the number three
three times imbedded
in its shell,
everyone else too sophisticated
to think it means anything,
except me, and I believe
in good fortune and bad,
waiting for my brother to die
and remembering,
remembering the saddest parts,

the good reunions.

IMAGINING THE BEAR

From my window,
I see and hear the commotion,
a company of birds on the lawn:
pileated woodpecker, oddly aground,
screaming in the brush,
a nuthatch scrambling upside down
on the trunk of a white oak,
sparrows hopping away in haste,
a thrasher dragging his tail
as if unable to fly.

I see no creature on chase,
only a huge tree trunk,
its uprooted end
looking like a giant bear claw
ready to pounce,
its secrets scattering on the wind.
And do these secrets disturb the air
swirling around the birds,
setting the leaves on wing?

I go outside and stand on the porch,
looking at the morning,
bright with promise.
The birds hush their exchanges,
take to the air,
leave me there in silent supplication,
asking, how could a tree root
disturb their places
among the shelter of trees?

Silently, I tell them:
You frightened birds,

be thankful for a dead tree
and its reposing feet,
its time had surely come,
the claw is only a gravestone,
mercy fallen on the withered grass,
and there is no world of error here —
this is God's disposition.

JEWELWEEDS

Orange diamonds lean over the trail,
glints of happiness that know
their place in the world,
no mystical botany for them,
no grasping for survival.
At home in the wild brush of forest,
they do not shout about righteousness,
are passionate without explanation,
their fiery blooms well named.

They nod at us to stop,
partake of love without danger,
not to look back at contradictions —
colors fading at fall's edge
inviting us to stake a claim
to this time, this summer light
slowly waning.

LARGE FAIRY RINGS BAFFLE SCIENTISTS

The moon is hiding,
waiting for the bleached air
to gather darkness,
waiting for the time
to send out fairies,
quicksilver on enchanted feet
making rings of bafflement
in the Namib Desert.

My mother believed in fairies,
would have said they dance
in a perfect ring
by the white light of the moon
while coyotes howl
and owls hoot,
to prove everything is magical
in the night,
the moon does its work
so we can cheat oblivion.

She painted these rings
knowing that years after
they would appear in Africa,
a few fairies that got away
from her soft brush,
knowing I would one day
recognize they had turned up
to part the dread and fear
that sometimes touch me
from oceans away.
Rings in a desert,
created by winged creatures

filled with grace,
fallen from the sky,
leaving their fairy dust
in a circle of love and safety
and, in the center,
a place to hope.

LEGACY

I sit by the window
opening on a memory of Mother;
She dances across a field of mud
transformed into a creature
with the head of a chicken,
the torso of a turkey,
legs of a duck,
and, oh yes, the mouth of a goose
babbling in rhyme
(and frowning at my free verse).

She sings the song of the churkendoose,
a recording she bought for us in 1948
and I, a tortured teenager,
played it endless hours,
this story about an odd barnyard animal
not a chicken, turkey, duck, or goose
but a combination of all forms,
singing about the perils
of facing "difference."

The churkendoose had only one ear
jutting from the back of its head,
could not walk,
but danced everywhere,
first appeared as an object of ridicule,
then became a hero because a fox,
intent on eating barnyard creatures,
entered the feathered domain
and, startled by the appearance
of the strange-looking churkendoose,
ran away so fast he flew backwards,
and his shadow didn't catch up for days.

The record became a leitmotif
for my tormented adolescence.
I played it over and over,
sang with it,
danced to the lyrics:
"It depends upon,
begins and ends upon,
it all depends on
how you look at things."*

Now I sit by the window
opening on a memory of Mother,
wondering,
How did Dorothy,
lover of fantasy and dreams,
know to transmit
this message about acceptance
without hurling moral lessons—
shoulds, dos and don'ts—
into our struggling psyches
so that one day
We'd still be humming lyrics
about the truth of love
sung by a quirky animal
in a tune celebrating
the triumph of "difference?"

* "The Churkendoose," Decca label, 1947

TELEVISION FARE

Sabbath afternoon of rest has passed,
dark television dramas watched,
eyebrows lifting
at film recording lost lives
and the pall of death,
phantoms with single names:
Betrayal, Revenge, Rectify,
and not-to-be-forgotten Scandal.

Stepping onto the porch,
you inhale ozone from thunderheads,
rain releasing a scent
of earth and plants,
and marvel that you are still alive
after that grim panoply
of television-grown demons,
the burden of crime.
Naked light bulb
dangles over a dead woman's body,
slayings lurk in the shadows
of monastery gardens,
hooded faces in black cloaks
knock at the front door,
prodigal victims of The Beast
who, in an excess of tension and lust,
flashed on a glowing screen,
Surreptitious having groomed herself
for an evening of blood and alarm.

You close your eyes,
postponing the effect,
three dark hours spent
as a breathless witness,

knowing you will be revisited
in night hours of soul-searching
by Betrayal, Revenge, Rectify
and not-to-be-forgotten Scandal
who joins the line of wickeds
and quickly undresses
behind closed doors.

TRIBES

In a mountain of stony silence,
the family Decadent carries
centuries of hate in its memory,
immune to its own violations.

Tribal hawks, savage and shrill,
live with appropriations and greed,
primitive thoughts aching in their heads.

Cordiality is unknown to them,
wasted breath, they say,
they live by cracker creeds,
cracker deeds,
ignoring guilt-ridden neighbors.

But they yearn for the good life —
for a shower of roses
to fall outside of themselves,
wondering how it feels
not to be gods, absolutely right,

how it is to look for light
beyond last winter's grievances,
a light that will converge
on their tragic history
so they can welcome the unknown,
escape the shadow of exclusion.

CONVERSIONS

We called it Pueblo In the Sand, the rude adobe hut in Old El Paso; a cheerless mud brick hovel the color of sand hidden behind a white frame house. Sand drifted under the door and wind blew at 30 miles per hour over the peaks of Mt. Franklin, the gusts fanning a strange religious fervor. I, a cradle Episcopalian, suffered a sudden, bizarre seizure, was baptized and confirmed Roman Catholic at the altar of the oldest mission in Texas — Ysleta Roman Catholic Church.

I had been a passenger who rode to work through early morning dust devils on a yellow school bus that stopped every block for chattering Chicanos to scramble aboard. I was eighteen years old, every Sunday gazing upward at Our Lady of Guadalupe standing on the head of a snake, believing she would rescue me from life in Pueblo In the Sand. Weeds grew up through the shower drain and red paint on tin walls peeled its blood into the long tendrils. A listless fan stirred stale air in our one-room hovel.

Adobe In the Sand was the first apartment we circled in the El Paso Times, having traveled non-stop from a Van Horn, Texas all-night station where the Plymouth sputtered and died and we traded it for a sleeker ride, a Mercury station wagon hiding a broken block that also sputtered and died after we moved north that winter.

We wondered at the perversity of the military naming the desert post "Fort Bliss" where the sky remained dry and unforgiving, and three hundred days of drought passed. In the fall, the command post sent orders transferring us to Limestone, Maine, the cold rim of an ice world. I looked out a smudged window at snow banking my loneliness in drifts high as telephone poles, trapped in the second story of an old farmhouse flaking gray paint.

That winter I fled to Confession on Saturdays, admitting apostasy without remorse, a French-Canadian priest assigning me ten Hail Mary's and hours on my knees to atone for my growing disbelief.

Oh, the contrariness of the Army matching heat with cold posts, loneliness and survival. Twin endurance. And eighteen months passed before I lost the religious fervor, returning to some distance from Rome and, too, from a bewitching wind that had blown a cloudy dogma into the Pueblo In The Sand and later buried it in a bank of snow.

A DAUGHTER'S SURGERY

I.

Doors open and close,
the air in long, icy halls
scented with antiseptic.
Someone cries behind a curtain
along the way,
patients shuttle in and out
of hidden rooms,
family names called
like patrons in a repair shop.
Your car is ready.
Tires rotated,
points and plugs inserted.
The motor may run sluggish
for a few weeks,
but come back
if you hear it missing.

The dazed swollen face
is wheeled into view
Of other dazed, swollen faces,
waiting.
Under the white fluorescence
the anemia of illness shines,
settles on one whose temporal body
has been drugged, carved,
and sent back to us.

God's handiwork has been revised,
indignities in every direction we look,
a form altered, skin patched,
new bondages created.

Our hearts, covered with gauze,
keep pressing the fountains of foam
dangling on walls of the long hall
as we follow the stretcher,
washing our hands at every station...
as if they had her blood on them.

II.

From my study window
the bright leaves of fall
flirt with the wind,
falling as they meet with gusts,
victims of brazen encounter.
The sun berates me
for failing to assume its brightness,
but I am held hostage
to my daughter's pain,
the curse of symbiosis,
54 years and still pleading
for health I did not give her,
for happiness severed
in one slash of the umbilical cord.
What chemistry of painful longing
ran counter to contentment?
a precarious state,
the child within her mother
traveling on a desperate journey
into the world.
Had I the mind of the One
Whom None Can Hinder,
heaven would rest
in every cell of her hungry body,
reflecting all that belongs
to the Creator,
the blood of health swift to flow
from the source of a river
in the just kingdom
where she could mingle
among the bright leaves
under a new sun,
unmoved by the wind.

III

THE ART OF SWEEPING

There was something about the comfort
of provincial stillness I felt
while sweeping Grandmother's front gallery.
But I was nine,
a quiescent stage, behavioral scientists say,
the calm of the known settling
into the slow hours of summer,
a sawmill up the street
humming a monotonous aria.

It was before the many steps ahead
and the arrival of by-and-by.

When I went outdoors to do the task,
bright as a morning butterfly
sweeping away the grains of dust
beneath the scaling swing
and from around the overflowing fern,
I learned a way I would remember
to rid the remains of future suffering,
the broom moving
across a splintered floor,
each whisk clouding the humid air,
and under the yellow needles —
the quiet of old dust.

A DREAM

The plumbing burst, and excrement drained into the house. We had been traveling in the mountains. A tenant in the apartment behind us sent a message of fury: *I am moving out*. When I arrived home, I found my brother Michael, who died one winter on the streets of Chicago. He had pitched a tent in the sodden leaves of my backyard, misfortune lying on old newspapers. I told him he could not live with me, and he begged for his life. *But you are dead*, I said. *No*, he said, *I only pretended. I swallowed tetrodotoxin and came back. I have been wandering five years*. I tried to banish him. I took down the tent poles, and his dwelling collapsed. It occurred to me he could clean up excrement in exchange for living with me. This would be my way of accepting responsibility for the life he could not control. He removed his street clothes, and I removed my shoes. In the sea of excrement we walked, a family bonded by waste—one sibling in a bare body, the other in bare feet, waist deep in madness, trying to clean up our lives.

PORTRAIT OF GREAT-GRANDFATHER

He appears to be gentle,
blue eyes peering from an oval frame,
not a wrinkle in the gray uniform.
He is tailored for action,
and in his eyes the presumption
of valor and glory shines.

Now on a cold November morning
he stares into the gloom
as if he'd never been imprisoned,
as if the Rebs hadn't lost
a battle General Grant won
while drunk the entire time.
Leaves fly in the wind
near Stone River,
tree trunks shaved off,
flies feasting on dead bodies.

He stares past the window
into another opening on Shiloh,
the blood-filled pond
where he washed his wounded leg,
Beauregard pushing them hard
toward Corinth Road.

And in the midst of carnage,
a pink dogwood blooms.

A bowtie is snug at the throat
of his white shirt,
brass buttons gleam,
a false show of victory;

he looks alive by some right
of Celtic renewal.

This is the portrait of a man
who came out of the fray
with no money, no profession,
a man at the bottom
of the Virginia class system,
as melancholy as he'd been
in the death pen at Ft. Delaware,
the threshold of hell.

He appears to be gentle
but I know where he has been,
see the blue eyes stirring,
his red hair afire
from some imprecation,
reminding me he was the first Captain
of our family's lost causes,
a torn flag fluttering
above the gold frame.

A BLESSING

Morning...
 a layer of frost shines
on rooftops across the way.

My oversized slippers lead the way
to the breakfast table,
my hands deep in the pockets
of a chenille robe showing its age.

Seven a.m. and the day is coiled
tight around the cold,
outdoors, crows call my name,
knowing the face at the window,
claiming a known territory
as they swoop over
the carpet of dry grass.

A skillet sizzles on the stove,
television blaring old news
about Israel and Palestine
carrying on another godless war,
false stroke upon false stroke,
parading like naked Emperors
in the name of Religion.

We sit at the dining table,
silver spoons on mats from Oaxaca City,
lift the lid of a white bowl
engraved with ceramic apples
and holding a gracious plenty,
unfold napkins that have been asleep
in a silver pitcher all night.

Opening a book of blessings,
we give thanks for homely objects,
banishing shadows created in the night.

We are hungry for life
and the disturbances of light
filtering through the blue sky
of Karen's glass art
suspended on the breakfast porch,
an anointing from the invisible world.
God's glance
bringing love home again.

NEW YEAR'S DAY

How can we celebrate
a new year filled with dense fog
wearing the shroud of an old man?
Birds, unseen, complain,
startled in their nests
by a sky overhanging mute trees.
The ghosts of cypresses
rise out of the marshes...
our rooms are dark at noon.

I long for a lively dog
to come to the door
and shake his fur,
so I can get up
and let him in
smelling of grass
and the damp earth;

for a streak of sunlight
to come to me alone,
a green leaf to unfurl;
for Greek gods to descend
on the gray clouds,
revising old histories in the mist,
changing people into objects
and more simple forms:
dragonflies, sunflowers, cardinals,
pine trees that can pray aloud,
stones that plead with wind
to change direction...
lift the impenetrable.

THE BRIDGE ACROSS BAYOU TECHE

When I first crossed the steel bridge
the murky stream beneath
appeared to be a fountain
that I would not dip into,
its day of commerce past.

Those born on its banks
told me right away
if I tasted this water
and moved away,
I would always return
to drink from it again.

That I'd not forget
small boats anchored
in the rank smell
of crabs and catfish,
cane poles concentrated
over slow-moving water,
mud turtles and scaled animals
lurking on a slimy bottom.

They tore down the old bridge
and I went away.
But I returned each year
to taste the water,
a revival of ancestral hope.

And in the brackish smelling air,
amid centuries of mist and water,
I crossed the new bridge to drop anchor
in sight of the carousing Teche...
stillness arriving

where blood had run deep.

TRACKS

The morning train
pants through
carrying the lonely past,
blasts a sharper whistle
in an unpredictable winter.
An old woman
wails for a future
while the wheels keep turning
toward the other side.

FOLLY

This morning I found three feathers
buried in leaves by the glass porch,
symbols of erratic flight,
a sparrow traveled off course,
plunged in rapid free fall,
a dive gone too far.

A fat gray cat strolls away,
flicking his whiskers,
no sign of struggling with desire,
no remorse in his appetite,
everything of substance vanished...
the gnarled fist of a bird's foot
clutching the driveway.

PONDERING MORTALITY AT MIDNIGHT

A dog barks at darkness,
the moon interloping his territory.
Prayers rise from my pillow
begging anxiety
to tighten the chain,
muffle his intrusion.

An old film shot
flashes across the white wall,
King David pacing a rooftop at night,
lamenting his love of Bathsheba.

Too many closed doors
hide black sheep of the past,
shadows undress in the window
of a bedroom devoid of stars.
A chill wind whips the curtains,
the yapping dog moves closer.

PASSING THE PASSING PARLOR,

The Evangeline Funeral Home,
I glimpse jovial sitters on the porch
marking time at the hotel of death,
place cards in the lobby,
drinks in the back room,
folks with *joie de vivre*
celebrating a passing.

The sweet smell of gladiolas
follows me to Winn Dixie
where I find orchids
scenting the bottles of salad dressing,
and outside an old woman with a cane
waits beside a small car,
"Sport" written on its sleek side,
in a parking lot already too full.
The hearse moving on
in spite of such predicaments.

FINALE

The settlement of leaves
is a monotonous brown outside,
brother finally died
and nothing is left
that won't blow away.
Fall has become the peace of winter.

He had my father's hands,
some notion of infinity
in the flowers he grew,
the only memory now,
the rustle of leaves,
a mute heap of ashes
in an urn without a window
or a stone to mark his passing.
And he will remain like that,
mild as a shadow on an old wall
getting a good night's sleep.

THE LOST COLONY OF RUGBY, TENNESSEE

Fog hovers over dark houses
but ghosts never sleep.
Absentee landlords disbelieve
souls are waiting to be released,
one murdered at the Tabard Inn,
another, a phantom librarian
who keeps sealed books
in an airtight room;
the Twin Oaks witch
and all the other safeguards
against modernity.

An English nobleman
worked with feverish speculation
to build this village,
create trades for ne'er-do-wells,
smallpox claiming unremarkable men
living in unused chambers —
a failed experiment.

Muffled voices carry on wind
whisking in a century
of invisible beings,
and I keep returning to this place,
as if some disturbing truth
is about to come forth,
that I will find them
staring out of the thick walls,
conspirators at old addresses,
trying to hold back time.

THE KILLING OF ERIC GARNER
(a teen-aged black male)

The cross of green gemstones
and sharp silver nails
gleams in the sunroom.

It is clear who hammered in the nails,
the shadow of a stranger
whimpering at the last,
Father, I cannot breathe;

black lamb locked in a chokehold
by white flesh without a heart,
dragged into fame's crucifix.

And now they riot in the streets.
Rabbis chant the Kaddish,
swarm around his tormentors
masked in blue uniforms,
police playing at their best game —
Reprisal.

No one on the crowded street
tells the executioners
their discourtesy
has made an indelible stain
and they should be careful —
fates could be joined together.

They are dressed for a parade
on a one-way street.
Justice limps off
hoping for one deep breath,
a hint of fresh air on the same street,

but without warning
falls in a pothole.

They cannot revive him.

EARLY PHONE CALL FROM A FRIEND SUFFERING DISAPPOINTMENT

What is it, she asked,
when all is aligned
in your universe
and the thing you desire
Doesn't happen?

An unforgiving gravity
pulls you down, I answer.
Nothing is really precise.
Luck sometimes wears a black hat
and bites with a sore tooth.

Those angel cards
you like to play
Don't always predict
deserved good fortune.

Happiness is often
sent into exile,
but don't bite your fingernails
over vanishing loss.

Hold hands with ambiguity
and sing the blues...
embrace the Cloud of Unknowing
when it hovers over you.

And outside, a lone crow
wheels in the winter sky

squawking more of the same:
If you knew,
you wouldn't dare...

HARVEST

Tiny mill hands scatter
in all directions,
immigrants combing
a glass porch's borders,
just come in from the rain
slowly falling on their ashy temple.

Out of poverty and thrift
they make ends meet,
create the world's
most passionate industry,

Ants & Company,
not in the Fortune 500,
but working day and night
to put bread on the table,
sending lookouts to canvass
our fallen daily crumbs.

Their feet scurrying,
lips unmoving,
they utter no sound
as they carry off
a multi-layered cake
surpassing all their exigencies...

And as they feast,
I suddenly remember a maxim
from picnics of the past:
"diligence is the mother of good luck."*

* From *The Way to Wealth* by Benjamin Franklin

CLOUDY AND COLD

Weather will finally bury us,
disturbing our world of assumption,
sheets of snow, rivers flooding,
the onslaught of our own making
and something beyond our making,

blizzards of caution unheeded,
the sun terminally ill,
and, us, a race inured to harnessing
the power we don't possess,
meddling with the heavens

as if we owned it all —
earth, sky, oceans, the wind
that blows a warning
across the prairie,
crawfish ponds, rice fields,
sugarcane swaying in a storm
predicting no harvest.

Weather will finally bury us,
shaking its fist in an uncertain sky,
and we will sink in a slough of remorse
wondering why we didn't trust
the weather vanes of our folly.

SNORING

The bed trembles.
terrified organs shudder:
heart pounding,
stomach rumbling,
vessels in the head constricting.
The place where panic lives
suddenly loses its grip
when hands raise
the blind on dreams,
and the mouth opens in song.

THE HORNS OF OUR DILEMMA

You can't escape suffering. It seems to have determined origins traced to an evolutionary theory that life in the present both transcends and includes the entire notebook of past events — the history of sentient human beings. And in the Now you are making you bring to each moment a black dog with heavy coat of fur while you attempt to create light in the world you know when a blank page rises before you already filled with the scribble of yesterday's weather.

IN ADDRESSING THE NEEDS OF
THOSE OBSESSING OVER THINNESS

and are unrecognizable
as their former fat selves,
a bit of didacticism gains voice:

Do you think Jesus worried
about the meals
for which he begged
and how they affected
the nutrition of his soul
or the sleekness of his body?
Oil, wine, matzo bread
spread with honey—
He heeded no diet hailed
as the miracle food of his day.

But He often had indigestion,
worrying about the sluggish arteries
of the soul: jealousy, hate, greed,
and the thin ones'
desire to kill fat people.
He preached the sovereignty of the soul
to Pharisees, Sadducees,
even the Essenes,
the latter, strict vegans
kneeling at their own
prie dieux of approval and censure.

And all those Hebrew keepers
legislating pork consumption,
their health obsessions hammering nails
into the hands of One who knew

the true meaning of nutrition.
He had plenty of customers
with their dark prophecies about food,
riding on the back of the Ass of Diet
and feeding on the fatback of judgment,
but they were unable to kill
the absolute weightlessness of love...
also known as the sovereignty of the soul.

CHANGING SEASONS

Rain pelts St. Francis
keeping watch on the patio,
his stone tonsure
split from the weather
of caring too much.
The winter has gone too far.

Above bronze pine straw
heaped around
the base of an oak
crows keep their distance,
crying for light;

At the edge of the coulee
the bellow of frogs drowns
in the noise of the noon train,
a line of passenger coaches
going East and North.

Storms came in the night.
A Christmas tree lies upended
at the end of the walk,
blown up from a yard
across the way,
now unadorned,
its empty boughs heavy
from a season's passing.

Safe indoors, I dream
of the forest's shawl
cloaking the Mountain at Sewanee,
gifts yet unopened
waiting for spring

when the modest dogwood
will drop its petals —
loveliness on ancient ground.

LEAVING THE LONELY GRANDMOTHER

She left the front door open to let in the south wind blowing that day. We sat in the living room, renewed by the meal she had cooked—fried chicken, butterbeans, rice, gravy, biscuits—a countrywoman's feast of grease and carbs and probably more food than she consumed in a month. But she had prepared the plenty because I was going back to Texas.

She had brought in the Emerson fan to reinforce the south wind, and it stirred up memories of long hours spent on the sleeping porch while the fan blew through the pages of books I read at nap time on summer afternoons. We could hear the phantom moving in the attic, the ghost I had seen when I was nine, but we both pretended we heard nothing.

The bust of Beethoven atop the bookcase looked down on us sitting there, our faces as stiff and expressionless as the marble features of the great musician. I had outgrown her. She had outgrown me. Only sentiment remained, thick as the cane syrup she had slathered on my breakfast pancakes when I visited in the summers and caused me to soil the green rug in the living room. I felt the need to throw off the tribal bands wrapped around us, and I knew she did too.

Yet, I couldn't bear to think of never sitting in the flaking green swing on the porch again. I held the hand of my own, a wriggling two-year old who had already made puddles on the same green rug I had christened. I stood and hugged my lonely grandmother, knocking her glasses askew on her nose. She readjusted them and looked at me out of eyes luminous with cataracts.

"Always wear something on your feet and legs so you won't

catch cold," she said.

"Yes ma'am."

"And teach that child how to use a potty chair. But tell her not to announce her bathroom habits."

"Yes ma'am."

The door was open. It was black and pebbled with age. And heavy. I remembered how hard it had been for me to open it when I was a child. I went out on the porch and looked down at the indentions of time passing—white marks the slat-backed rockers had left on the porch from years of lonely rocking.

She closed the heavy door behind me. When I reached the sidewalk, I looked up at the cupola on the roof of the old house. A phantom flew out of the window beneath it and disappeared in the sky.

TWENTY-SEVEN DEGREES

Crows protest the cold,
screaming in their perch
on fingers of the pine.
Frozen by their strident cries
the branches snap,
black wings flap into empty space,
courting exile.
They taste frost,
see me sitting at the window
wearing a black sweater,
think of me as brethren
on this funereal day.

People cross the churchyard
dressed in black robes,
complaining about the closed sky.
The crows move nearer,
crying for red wine,
a feast table,
an evening fire.
They want to steal my sweater,
join a procession of Arctic explorers.

At my desk I see
the window needs cleaning
before winter ends,
before the crows break in
to take me hostage,
hurrying me into nowhere
to be a bit player
in one of their dark tableaus,
where I would walk out
stuttering on the alien word:

Obscurity.

ABOUT THE AUTHOR

Diane Marquart Moore is the author of books, short stories, articles, and poetry. Her poetry and short stories have appeared in *The Southwestern Review* a journal of the University of Louisiana at Lafayette, *Interdisciplinary Humanities, The Xavier Review, American Weave, Louisiana Historical Review, Trace, Pinyon Review, Acadiana Profile Magazine,* and other literary journals. Her young adult book, *Martin's Quest,* was awarded a grant that placed it on the supplementary reading list for Social Studies in Terrebonne and Lafourche parishes and was a finalist in the Heekins Foundation Award Contest for an outstanding young adult book. Diane is a former Associate Editor of *Acadiana Lifestyle* magazine in New Iberia, Louisiana and was a feature writer and columnist for *The Daily Iberian* in New Iberia. She was also a feature writer for The *Yaddasht Haftegy* in Ahwaz, Iran where she lived for two years during the reign of the Shahanshah. She divides her time between New Iberia, Louisiana and Sewanee, Tennessee.

www.ingramcontent.com/pod-product-compliance
Lightning Source LLC
Chambersburg PA
CBHW062019040426
42447CB00010B/2069